Dear Kaylie,
   Delighted to have such a lovely neighbor buy my book — thank you.
   I hope you enjoy it.
   God bless you all-ways!
      Sandy Robinette

OF THINGS VISIBLE AND INVISIBLE

Poems and Essays

SANDY ROBINETTE

WESTBOW PRESS®
A DIVISION OF THOMAS NELSON
& ZONDERVAN

Copyright © 2020 Sandy Robinette.

All rights reserved. No part of this book may be used or reproduced by any means, graphic, electronic, or mechanical, including photocopying, recording, taping or by any information storage retrieval system without the written permission of the author except in the case of brief quotations embodied in critical articles and reviews.

This book is a work of non-fiction. Unless otherwise noted, the author and the publisher make no explicit guarantees as to the accuracy of the information contained in this book and in some cases, names of people and places have been altered to protect their privacy.

WestBow Press books may be ordered through booksellers or by contacting:

WestBow Press
A Division of Thomas Nelson & Zondervan
1663 Liberty Drive
Bloomington, IN 47403
www.westbowpress.com
844-714-3454

Because of the dynamic nature of the Internet, any web addresses or links contained in this book may have changed since publication and may no longer be valid. The views expressed in this work are solely those of the author and do not necessarily reflect the views of the publisher, and the publisher hereby disclaims any responsibility for them.

Any people depicted in stock imagery provided by Getty Images are models, and such images are being used for illustrative purposes only. Certain stock imagery © Getty Images.

Cover Art and Interior Sketches: ©Lily Robinette
Author photo: ©CRobinette

Scripture quotations are taken from the New American Bible, St. Joseph Edition. Copyright © 2010, 1991, 1986, 1970 Confraternity of Christian Doctrine, Inc., Washington, DC. All Rights Reserved.

ISBN: 978-1-6642-0358-7 (sc)
ISBN: 978-1-6642-0359-4 (e)

Library of Congress Control Number: 2020916373

Print information available on the last page.

WestBow Press rev. date: 09/24/2020

AMDG

DEDICATION
To my family and friends
For their love, prayers, and support
All-ways!

PSALM 121
verse 1 and 2

I raise my eyes toward the mountains.
From where will my help come?
My help comes from the Lord,
the maker of heaven and earth.

©St. Joseph Edition of
The New American Bible (NAB)

TABLE OF CONTENTS

HELLO, DEAR READER!. 1
SELF PORTRAIT 3

LOVE. 7

SAINT PAUL AND MY HUSBAND 9
HELLO. 11
HISTORY OF A KISS 13
SAD SONGS 15
LOVE IS EASY 17
PASSION AND AGE 19

CHILDREN 21

LAVABO, A PRAYER 23
MY SON RUNS AWAY. 25
WELL LOVED SON 27
PHARISEE KNEES 29

ENCOUNTERS WITH THE SPIRIT 31

AFTER THE NEW YEAR 33
ON THE FEAST OF PENTECOST 35
SEARCH FOR HUMILITY 37
MY PRAYER FOR LOST THINGS 39
MEDITATION ON PAIN AND HEAVEN. 41

YOU AND ME 43
SIMPLE TRUTH 45

WEATHER WISDOM 47

A PAUSE FOR WONDER. 49
THE WEATHERMAN 51
SPRING 53
BEACH SCENE 55
MY HANGING CRYSTAL 57
WIND. 59
SCIENTISTS BEWARE. 61
ROSE PETALS 63
WINDOWS OPEN 65
WEATHER REPORTS 67
HARVEST MOON 69

LET ME TELL YOU A LOVE STORY 71

LOVE LATER 73
LET ME TELL YOU A LOVE STORY 75
TRAVEL SONG 79

GRIEF. 81

DEATH WATCH 83
GOODBYE, LOVE. 85
A TRILOGY OF GRIEF 87
WIDOW. 91

LONELY..93
REMEMBERING...................................95

AGE AND THE EVERYDAY......................97

SOME DAY...99
BEDTIME STORY................................. 101
SENIOR MEETING................................ 103
SPRING CLEANING 105
AMEN ROSES 107

HISTORY 109

JAMESTOWN 2007 111
JAMESTOWN 1607 – 2007........................ 113
FOURTH OF JULY 115
THE GREAT DISMAL SWAMP FIRE 117
FRED HEUTTE, I LOVE YOU 121
FREDERIC HEUTTE (1899 – 1979)................ 125

FINAL THOUGHT..............................127

WHY WRITE?......................................129
ABOUT THE AUTHOR............................ 133

HELLO, DEAR READER!

You **are** dear to me. You picked my book to invest your time in exploring. My hope is that this decision to join me will offer you new insights on the reality before our eyes and the life of the Spirit which wraps around us, just out of sight.

Written over several decades of my life, these poems and essays are reflections on living my faith in real time. Subjects range from marriage and children to heartbreak and grief. The many faces of love. Even a late life romance. I like to think there is a lot of sunlight too and some laughs.

I write from a Roman Catholic perspective because this is my faith, my consolation, my joy, my home. I have not always served the church well and I am a sinner. I have doubted and questioned often and found the way, the truth, and the life in Jesus. That is one reason I love my Church.

Jesus welcomes sinners and I find Him in the abundant grace offered in the sacraments of the Catholic Church, especially the Holy Eucharist. My Catholic Church is the body of Christ alive now and trying to do God's work.

I believe that Jesus is the Son of God, who lived as one of us, loved like one of us, was betrayed and died horribly on the Cross for my sins. He is risen and now acts as my brother in heaven until we are united for all eternity. The Holy Spirit keeps us connected.

You may not agree with me but perhaps you will find a new dimension of ideas that might deepen your own faith life. As my last poem notes, you are in charge because you are the reader.

I welcome your company on this journey.

Sandy Robinette
2020

SELF PORTRAIT

I see my face in the mirror
And do not recognize myself.
What happened to me?

I see the flash of round cheeks,
An upsweep of baby hair,
Captured in a spotted old photo.

Another newer one,
The graduate in cap and gown,
Smiling with joyful success,
Proud of me.

Wedding pictures with floral crown,
A bride waiting, in demure white eyelet,
With no idea of what is to come.

Years full of pictures, boxes brimming,
Of me and him, me and them,
Mostly them, the children.

Shining babies, toddlers off on adventures.
The mighty conqueror on his first bike,
Let go to pedal away, aware of speed
For the first time.

Flashing a smile to celebrate that first fish,
Finger size to become a legend in the telling.

Girl children in Easter hats and shiny new shoes.
Boys with slicked down hair, shirts tucked in,
Bow ties clipped to collars, hands in pockets –
Tidy for a few brief moments.

Smiles and trophies,
Dirt and disappointment,
More weddings, more babies.
A documentary of love, life.
Visiting, going, coming, loss, hurt,
Forgiveness, work, play, and
Deaths, so many dead.

Now that face created
Looks back at what is left.
Hair gray, shading into white,
The outward sign of winter within.

The lines in patterns,
Crisscrossed on cheeks,
More from smiles than frowns,
I like to think.

The thinning lips of age,
With lines drawn along the edges,
To record kisses, many kisses,
Given and returned.

But my favorite is the eyes,
Still pale blue,
With lines from lid to brows,
For the times, the many times,
I looked wide-eyed at my world,
In wonder and joy.

Amazed by love and life …
My face after all,
Earned in the living.

For Ellie Newbauer, Poet and Wise Woman
2019

Love

SAINT PAUL AND MY HUSBAND

"I love a good man…"
The song wails along.
What is a good man to love?

I loved a good man
Who brought a meeting
Of the mind as well as the body,
And kindness.

That much underrated
Virtue.
The virtue that defies science
Because it oils friction
So that passion
Can ignite again and again.

Paul said it in a letter …
Love is patient, love is kind…*
Easy to say, Paul,
But wonder filled to live.

*1 Corinthians 13:4 (NAB)

HELLO

Someone says hello
And what happens?
Is it a love story
With fifty years
Of loving joy?

Is it just a moment
That flips the lips
From down to up?

A brief shift
And the world looks
Brighter?

One word, one smile –
Moments when
The whole world changes.

2007

HISTORY OF A KISS

That first kiss
is such a wonder.
Not bristled like my Dad.
His smooth, spicy cheek
to my cheek,
soft lips growing
sweeter, more insistent
with each second.

In time, all others forgot,
our kiss explodes
in the marriage bed
so long awaited.
Passion
just being learned,
prelude to our own
thousand nights.

Kisses long,
Kisses quick.
A treasure,
easy comfort,
trigger to desire,
patch over anger.
Love
without words.

And at the end,
when breath is gone,
but not our love,
a tender touch, lip to lip.
Memories of all
the years of living –
quiet, rich simple
in one last goodbye kiss.

2003

SAD SONGS

I like sad songs.
Songs that
Recognize
That happy
Needs
'not'
To be
Appreciated.

You only know peace
After the anger;
After the storm;
After the bitter;
After.

Happy
Means sad
Didn't win.

That the heart
Included it
And broke
Into bigger.

Finding the world
Big and dark

And painful
Heals
When light,
Joy, and love perfect
The awful other.

LOVE IS EASY

Love is easy
For soft skinned limbs
And strong young arms.
When the slip and slide
of sex needs no coaxing.
Kissing lips cling sweetly
Until yielding and opening.

Love is easy
When it's laughter and curling
Close in the marriage bed.
Moonlight making covers –
Sunshine waking you
To tender gentle nibbling,
A morning feast for lovers.

But love wears out,
Bare as an unpatched shirt;
Or grows stronger than steel
When life clutters your days
With earnings, yearnings,
Babies, toys, jobs, and things.

The rhythm of happy no longer meshes.
With each struggle to balance,
You keep learning to walk
An uneasy tightrope.

Love is easy
When you reach toward that known
Hand taking yours on the other side.

2019

PASSION AND AGE

A certain age
Signals no cessation of passion.

The young know nothing
Of the glory of sustained love
Or the bitter icy ache
Of long-time anger and hate.

Age burnishes the passions.
Strips away the false notions,
The non-essential, extraneous,
Unexamined and untrue,
leaving a nugget of something precious
or unfeeling at its frozen core.

Passion old is refined and scoured
Turned this way and that.
Self-consciousness rubbed off
Until clarity joins love
Or discovers darkness filled with rage.

Passion and age,
Age and passion.

Enriched with tears,
Still not always wise,
But embracing life for living,
Filled with overflowing giving,
Or strangled in ne'er forgotten lies.

Sandy Robinette, "Passion and Age," in **The Poet's Domain**, *volume twenty-three, edited by Patricia S. Adler. (Live Wire Press, Charlottesville, Virginia, 2008), 133.*
All rights returned to the author.

Children

LAVABO, A PRAYER

God, see us
From your dwelling place.

Here is mine, hoping to reflect you
In sofa, chair, and pictured wall –
A little of that waiting splendor.

Let iniquity with red hands,
Whispered bribes, gossip face,
Live not our neighbors.

But purified amid the tricycles,
Splashed in shiny baby laughter
In the colors of the baby pool,
I wash my hands in innocence
And wash theirs too.

Encompassing your glory
In soapy bubbles,
Drenched in chiming children,
I wash.

A note of explanation:

LAVABO means *wash* in Latin. I know it from the Celebration of the Mass as the prayer the Priest says as he actually washes his hands to cleanse himself from sin. Then he moves into the Eucharistic Prayer at the heart of the Mass.

Finding joy and love in the innocence of children and the simplicity of a bath became a prayer of thanks and a prayer for help against the household sins of pride and envy and gossip that have no place near "my chiming children".

Written long ago:

Revised, January 2, 2020

MY SON RUNS AWAY

What happened?
I don't feel anything.
I'm not even angry anymore.
That's burnt up and ash now.

But my boy is gone,
Not here, or anywhere
That I know of.
I still feel empty –
Nowhere, no one.
I didn't run away and yet I'm gone.

What happens when he returns?
Nothing is changed and everything.
Will he really be here again?
Will my inside outside self return?
Who will I be then?

November 1974

WELL LOVED SON

I love my son beyond words.
Every heartache
Has been redeemed
Ten times ten.
Prodigal son.

Every stressed mother,
And father perhaps,
Whose survivor son
Stretches out a hand,
Returning.

A loving hand, caress,
A hug...
A bulwark now against
The cold and winds of old.

2010

PHARISEE KNEES

Pharisee that I am
I want to be seen
As knowing what to do –
In church, at least.

There aren't many places
Where I am considered
An expert any longer.
(If I ever was,
But that's another poem.)

Now I'm at church kneeling
And standing and singing –
Heaven help us.
But, having fallen and
Knelt abruptly on a tile floor,
My knees complain in pain.

It is hard to sit here,
At least to my church proper mind.
I want to put a sign around my neck.
"My knees hurt."
A justification for failing that norm
In my head.

I remember telling
My teen-age son
To kneel up.
He said his knees hurt.

"Offer it up.
If you can't pray,
Your body can."

Forgive me, dear boy,
Now a robust man in his prime,
Whose knees still hurt.

Encounters with The Spirit

AFTER THE NEW YEAR

The holly days
are over,
although my prickly plant
still hangs its berries
In red clusters.

The stars of
Christmas
give way to
a deep mysterious
nightly shimmer.

The chatter of
bells and song
quiet into
meditation
and silence.

Now is the
holy season
when the mysteries
work their way
into real life.

*Sandy Robinette, "After the New Year", in **Skipping Stones**, edited by Pete Freas and Anne Meek. (Mindworm Press: Chesapeake, Virginia, 2006), 11. All rights retained by author.*

ON THE FEAST OF PENTECOST

Holy Spirit,
The Force in a life realized,
Who takes my sluggish faith
And pushes, pokes, and propels
My mild affection for good
Into something alive and potent.

Unless I neutralize you
With reasonable doubt and
Careful inaction, deciding to take a nap.

Was I sleeping
When the tongues of flame
Were lighted?
Or maybe too relaxed with wine,
To hear the wind, to feel its chill
And blaze with joy?

2014

SEARCH FOR HUMILITY

Being right.
The headiness of
Knowing it all
Degenerates into
Holding up my ego
More than seeking
The truth.

It's the difference between
A Jeopardy contestant
Who has all the answers
And the wise and humble
Person
Who has the patience
To seek the whole truth.

That realization
Gives me pause
To consider the
Possibility someone else
Knows more true
Than me.

That being right
Is a sin.
Entrenched pride

As virtue,
Subtle perversion,
Respectable evil.

Be open instead,
Because it's not about me.
Repent and find
A clean heart;
Be open to the mystery
Of grace,
The truth of
Holy uncertainty.

2020

MY PRAYER FOR LOST THINGS
(and SOULS)

Saint Anthony, Saint Anthony
Please come around
Something is lost and
Cannot be found.

Saint Anthony, Saint Anthony,
Gracious saint,
Open my eyes to the obvious.
What I seek
Is so often right
In front of me, again.

Why can't I see it?
How many ordinary
Blessings have I missed
Because I couldn't,
Wouldn't,
See them?

Saint Anthony of Padua was a Franciscan priest of the 13th century. St. Francis of Assisi himself sent Anthony throughout Italy because of his amazing preaching of the Gospel.

He died at the age of thirty-six but, in his brief life, he left a legacy of thought so rich and good that he was declared a Doctor of the Church.

I found pictures of artwork showing many statues of him. He stands in his brown habit, young and smiling, in all of them.

He was known not only for his preaching but also for finding things.

MEDITATION ON PAIN AND HEAVEN

Is heaven that exquisite balance
Of pain and joy
Such as childbearing and birth?

The pain, discomfort, giving over of your
Body, to contain, at quite an
Inconvenience to yourself, a person.
As your belly grows, the baby begins
To fight for space with your organs,
Particularly the bladder.

Your body resembles a giant
Turnip, an eggplant of life.
A new idea of womanhood
And a subtle joy
In being female, fecund,
The mother container of life.

Old women, whisper, and
The helpful sort tells you
About the pain to come –
Stories to reveal the awe of the business.

Remembering perhaps
That they too were
Once vessels of creation,
full primal woman.

When the inevitable pain –
the wet, the blood,
The sweat, the smells,
The return to the same
Place as the first woman.
Our primitive ancestor,
Half human female
Delivering her young.

Life fighting out of your
Beautiful nest of a body
To the raw air, the
Cold breath of a new reality,
The wonder unknown life.

Life everlasting.
When woman, child and
God combine in creation,
Imprint on all three
Of heaven.

Easter 2019

YOU AND ME

I was wondering who God is?
Just like people have for untold years.
And talked about for years
If you read the Bible studies way.
Lots of answers there but what about God
In my today?

Is he that slightly scruffy Jesus
of stage and screen?
All those zippy songs do ring true
But each is too little to hold
Even my tiny experience of you.

Are you that mythic existence,
That Lion, not a tame lion?
That grandeur that I love in Lewis,
Who so helps me believe
On this skim of human hubris.

What has the Bethlehem Baby to do
With my here and now?
The Magi recognized his face
And left the family gifts.
Herod knew and killed the boy babies.
Would God plan that I would know this grace?

How dare I even think
About YOU
In any part of my experience?
How can me and YOU
BE at all?
But YOU and me ring true too,
Such a small sound but right.

How do you live crazily
With the sun?
You take the hand of the Son!
I am afraid to burn
And afraid not to.
I offer my fears of knowing
YOU.
And the joy.

Written yesterday

SIMPLE TRUTH

I have finally come to this –
a penitent heart.

I receive all the love
Given
But undeserved;
Unmerited,
Careless in acceptance,
Undervalued,
And my salvation.

I know now
I have never been alone.
I walk in clouds of angels
With Jesus by my side.

For the few whiles I have left,
He will be there in the
Dark valley of death
And in the light of every day.
And I will know He is,
Has been and is always
Because He loves me.

2020

Weather so often affects our internal barometer. "Rainy days and Mondays ..." come to mind. Snow followed by joyful shouts of 'no school'. Fog horns on the river set a special mood in my mind – if I don't have to drive in it. Weather wraps around our life, invisibly.

Weather can be as benign as sunshine on the seashore or as dangerous as wind whipping waves over the shoreline and destroying everything in its path.

Maybe it is the unpredictability of weather, despite all the attempts to look at the invisible factors and come up with a forecast. And the power and the glory of it. Whose power? Whose glory?

Weather Wisdom

A PAUSE FOR WONDER

The caldera of the volcano, Kilauea, on the Big Island of Hawai'i, stunned my senses.

Volcanoes National Park has wonderful Park Rangers who tell you the story of the volcano and its status – active! An exhibition explains the facts if you don't want to listen to the ranger. Another room is set up with a dozen or so seismic monitors with rolling scrolls of paper; pen-like markers recording the movements in the earth's crust under our feet. Scratching the ups and downs that mean changes under the crust.

Then you venture along the rim of the volcano and go down into the actual caldera. This crater is what happens after a volcano erupts and collapses. It is a ceiling over what lies beneath. This is a big deal! The caldera covers a large area, like a gray field of cinders and dirt.

Many feet trace the path, weaving among the cracks that allow steam to shoot into the air for a foot or two, or sometimes just a wisp floating up. I bent over to touch the ground and it was hot. Clearly I was close to the heated magma under my feet. It was a very disturbing sensation. Too close to those elemental forces for me!

Along the paths were piles of stones and something else. Offerings. I saw a large leaf with fruit and flowers arranged on it, and others with money added; a gift to the power of the volcano, personified by Pele. This power in the earth is a worthy place to pray and recognize a higher power.

In a recent eruption (1918), which destroyed 600 structures on the island, the volcano spewed lava that also created 250 acres of new land for the island. Pelehonuamea, she who shaped the sacred land, deserves notice.

THE WEATHERMAN

Like the weatherman
standing at his charts,
many colors moving,
swirling, seeming chaos
the evidence of wind and rain.

Is the Holy Spirit -
Our God of life and power,
moving in this storm of color,
warping around space with grace;
impatient to move us, hold us
in holiness?

Color me one with Father, Mother,
Son and You.

2018

SPRING

It's a perfectly nice day –
All blue sky and sunshine,
Until the wind blows in
Wildly dusting the earth,
Like a kid throwing sand
At the beach.

Let's sing and dance with it!
Wave our arms
Lose our hats
Welcome wild hair
Swirling skirts
Blossoms covering the car.

Beauty is brief.
This moment,
Like no other,
Never to come again.

BEACH SCENE

The ocean lips the shore
Tickling toes,
Long rollers slow motion
Lift the waiting surfers' boards.

The sun, the sand –
Beach paradise.

Beyond the blue-hazed horizon
Lurks the vast sea;
Waters, deep, seething,
The chop and turbulence,
The sullen heave.

Surging liquid power
Just at the edge of sight.

Sandy Robinette, "Beach Scene", in **Skipping Stones**, *edited by Pete Freas and Anne Meek. (Mindworm Press: Chesapeake, Virginia, 2007), 3. All rights retained by author.*

MY HANGING CRYSTAL

Spring sun angles a kiss
On my crystal,
Hanging in the window.

Rainbows splash and shatter
Across the walls,
Magic everywhere.

An eyelash move of earth and sun
As daylight mutes,
moves on.

Memory holding.

WIND

The mystery of weather –
Daily teacher of simplicity
And maximum complexity.

Listen to the weather people:
Wind direction, speed,
Highs, lows,
The mathematics of the
Roaring drafts of air.
All the calculus of the unseen.

I laugh as joy –
Also unseen, also real –
Ruffles my hair,
Blows my scarf,
Toys with my mood,
Until I smile.

Redeeming a day of despair,
With the certitude that this is
No random comfort –
But a gift of the Spirit.

SCIENTISTS BEWARE

"I only believe what I can see
Or weigh or measure ..."
So, what about wind?
No meteorologist has ever
Held that in a hand.
But every day, every hour,
You check for velocity, direction.
Anything else you can
never see.

Electricity is another unseen.
A gush of something.
Power to light the night,
Drive the energy of cities,
only seen in its results,
From lightning to spark.

Why would you doubt
That creation unseen
May be the mystery
That pursues you;
Invites you to wonder;
Pushes you to your knees.

In the face of such fire –
Worship the Maker!

ROSE PETALS

I bought a house
With a rose bush.

Glorious petals
Strew my front step.
I feel like a bride
As I walk to the car.

Small fragrant blessings –
Such little things,
Color, shape, scent.

Do I decorate my world
With gifts as welcome?
If I grew on your doorstep,
Would you and I rejoice
In beauty and love?

Sandy Robinette, "Rose Petals", in **Skipping Stones**, *edited by Pete Freas and Anne Meek. (Mindworm Press: Chesapeake, Virginia, 2006), 149. All rights retained by author.*

WINDOWS OPEN

My aging ears
Fill with static,
Electronic whine.

What happened
To the rain?

When I was young,
I would open my window
At night
And listen to the family of rain …

Drop by drop
In warming spring;
Splats and spits
Before the summer
Thunderstorm.

The drumming fists
Of fall
Met winter's sharp icy edge,
Softening to snow.

Now I hear memories
Better than
The rain.

Sandy Robinette, "Windows Open," in **The Poet's Domain**, volume twenty-six, edited by Patricia S. Adler. (Live Wire Press, Charlottesville, Virginia, 2010), 81.
All rights returned to the author.

WEATHER REPORTS

Climate changing
Or just the tempest?
Waves of water flowing
Through Ocracoke Island,
Houston, New Orleans,
My garage.

Winter in the Rockies–
Four feet of snow in September.
Ninety degrees on my thermometer,
Breaking records.
Hot in Raleigh.

Climate Question?
If it happens twice,
In two years
On the hundred year plain...
Are we safe now
For two hundred years?

Crazy me to believe
In climate change.

2019 September

HARVEST MOON

Hello, Moon,
Companion of my loneliness –
round and golden,
near, dear, almost warm.

Yet already clouds,
like a feather boa,
begin to drift
across your face.

Pale now, silvering
in the sky,
until it's just
the moon.

Sandy Robinette, "Harvest Moon", in **Skipping Stones**, *edited by Pete Freas and Anne Meek. (Mindworm Press: Chesapeake, Virginia, 2006), 156. All rights retained by author.*

Let me tell you a love story ...

LOVE LATER

The heart that loves
Will be broken.
The broken heart
Can be healed
In the tears that fall.

That heart can love again;
More careful, maybe.
More hesitant, maybe.
But also more.

LET ME TELL YOU A LOVE STORY ...

I was tending a table of books on Catholic life in the social hall of church after Mass on Sunday morning. This was a project sponsored by the Adult Faith Formation group to gauge interest in a Parish Library. Gregarious as ever, I was corralling my friends and acquaintances into borrowing a title or two.

My daughter and a friend were enjoying coffee and donuts while they watched me. A man I had not met stopped and looked around. "Do you need more books?" he asked. "Always," I said. He brought up a couple of titles that would be good additions; he smiled and left.

A few weeks passed and he stopped by now and then, although no books appeared for donation. He finally introduced himself and asked my name. As I was loading the books onto a rolling shelf to put back in storage, he said, "Would you consider having lunch or even dinner with me?" I felt comfortable enough to answer, "Yes." He smiled and left!

Well, life goes on and I was out of town for the next weekend. My daughter filled in for me with the books. When I returned, she called me up and let me know what she thought about "that man". He had stopped by the table and asked her where

I was. "Grilled me," she said. "After lurking like that all those weeks before."

This was the first I had heard about lurking! It seems that he had been sitting with some people having coffee every week and always sat where he could see me, but a little bit behind a column so I could not see him. Lurking. Did I notice him? No. Did she? Yes!

He persisted and said hello as soon as I put the books out the next week and asked me when I was available for lunch. I thought about it and decided we needed a more private place for this conversation. I gave him my phone number and asked him to call me. He did write it down and waved and …left!

He called and we scheduled lunch at a lovely restaurant. We talked and ate and talked and stayed most of the afternoon. So began our courtship.

He was a widower. I was a widow. Lots to talk about there. He had five daughters. I have eight children. That didn't scare him off. He came from a family of nine. I thought he was bright and dapper. I loved that he wore hats to church. He thought I was interesting. On such things, love flourishes.

We began to spend time together and it was noticed. *"Lunch with Hal, again?" "Who is it you're going to meet at the Chrysler Museum?" "You're looking happy!"*

I was. He was. Very happy when we were together. So pleased with each other that when he asked me to marry him, I said "yes". And, with that, he saved my soul.

I was in a situation that involved money, disappointment, and blame all around. It was consuming me with anger - bitter, hateful, and strong. I was telling my daughter how angry I was one day and suddenly realized how sick and evil I sounded. I had to stop or be damned by it.

Hal came as a gift to me to shine his goodness like sunshine into my life. Seeing myself clearly in that light gave me the strength to step back from the situation and let others resolve it. I am forever grateful, then and now.

He told everyone I saved his life, so maybe that thanked him in a special way. Before we were married, Hal called and said he was not feeling well and couldn't go to dinner as we had planned. His voice sounded as if he was gargling with pebbles. Then he started coughing and could not stop. He hung up. The sound of that cough echoed in my ears as I collected some chicken soup and crackers and orange juice and drove into Norfolk to his place.

I opened the backdoor and called his name and heard more coughing. That started hours of trying tea and soup, cough drops and anything else to diminish that awful sound. It was after midnight when I gave up. "Either you get your wallet and I drive you to the ER or I'm calling 911?"

He didn't argue and we went to the ER. The triage nurse heard him start coughing and he was whisked back to the treatment area in minutes. I negotiated my way in as his fiancé and was allowed to sit with him between oxygen and x-rays and IVs and finally admission to the Pulmonary Center. "Acute bronchitis but not yet pneumonia. Good thing you came in, especially with a man of his age."

Which brings up the subject of age and what were we doing? We were head over heels in love at the ages of 83 and 77. Did we know what we were doing? Between us, we had about 93 years of marital experience, and yes, we thought we knew what we were doing. We knew we would be lucky to have a decade together.

We married in 2015 and he died in 2018. We had a total of three years together.

It was a holy, happy, blessed decision.

TRAVEL SONG

Thank you,
Hal of my heart,
For giving me
New York.

The busy, the bustle,
The Carnegie Deli,
Giant corned beef
Sandwich.

Shoving, sinking
Into the throb
And movement
Of the city.

Mass in the
Glorious beauty of
St. Patrick.
Shopping Macy's flagship.

The museum marathon
Of stunning art,
New and old;
Time traveling
Cloisters.

Architecture –
The elegant sweep
Of the Chrysler Building;
Familiar, clever brick
At Carnegie Hall.

Rain, subways,
Damp horses at
The springtime park,
Hidden streets.

The Ritz,
The Plaza,
Morton's Grocery,
The Hamburger Joint.

Homeward bound
As the wheels roll
Back to our slow
Southern pace …
But there is
Nothing
Like New York!

May 2016

Grief

DEATH WATCH

Watching your husband,
Your love,
Endure the pain
Throughout his body.

I can only kiss
His lips and tip of nose,
Lightly, briefly,
Whispers of loving passion.

Lying in the kind bed
From hospice,
He suddenly explodes
Into flailing arms,
Legs kicking.

A last ditch fight
To stay
In the realm of pain?
At least familiar,
Tended by hands he knows.

Or desperate to find his way
To that gate or door
To forever more?

GOODBYE, LOVE

The love that is patient
And kind
Comes into the open
Or gets left behind.

Because love is hard now.
No fun, no champagne.
No fizz in the bloodstream,
Just the birth and the pain.

But love forged in the fires
And hells of small deaths
Is a love renewing,
not old love bereft.

A love bright as sunshine,
No longer sunk in grim dark;
hot anger dissolved 'til
sweet death docs us part.

RIP

A TRILOGY OF GRIEF

GRIEF, new

Two years, nine months, six days.
Widow.
The world I was living in,
Collapsed, gone.
I cannot return.
I live, he died -
And all our togethers stopped.

Loving words whispered
So often in the dark,
Now echoes of our passion,
Of our forevers.
Silent with no ear to hear.

Memories instead of kisses;
Holding hands, alone.

GRIEF & REGRETS, six months

Too short.
Our time was too short
To know
What I should apologize for;
To ask for his apologies.
So we both could understand
The other.

We planned too little, too late,
And time ran out.
The end too soon, too soon.
No small sin to waste it.

GRIEF & PEACE, one year

I've come to this place
In my heart again.
Gray fog hangs
Over everything out there
And in here too.

You know the future is close
From the beginning.
Love still takes the chance
That we – at least –
Will push the limit.
Not this time.

My memories will have to
Fill these longing years –
The reality remaining
A shadow of the intensity
Of loving.

Finally, I rest
Even though the room is empty.

This "Trilogy of Grief" was awarded second place in the Poetry competition at Hampton Roads Writers Conference in 2019. This is the first time it has been published.

WIDOW

I live, he died.
I must find my way
And go on,
Borrowing strength from
My family,
My friends,
Sharing sorrow.

The tears wash away
The heat of anger;
Humbling insights
Of lost chances to love.

My memories
hold the seed
Of that lovely beginning
As well as the blooming
Of life together.
Then the dark parts
Of illness
And good-bye.

Remembered love
To last me
To my blessed ending.

LONELY

Lonely is a new land.
Stranded by death
Of a friend,
A spouse,
Idea,
Or dog.
Each a unique alone.

The landmarks
Change,
And the familiar
Of life.
Family
New friends,
Panting puppies.
Rearrange.

Pray for the living
And the dead.

REMEMBERING

Time. Does it heal?
Remembering
At first is all sharp
Visions of the
Grim reality of death
Or loss or old joy.

At night in dreams
Or that half awake
Clarity that
plays the film of
Life – re-lived.

The memory details
Every act, every word,
Sigh, nuance of look,
Your response of love
Or something else.

As days and nights pass,
Each remembrance
Becomes a little less clear,
As if your nose and fingers
Pressed against a window
Blurring details.

Your inner ear hears
The whispered words of love,
More faintly.
The bleeding sounds of
Anger fade like a
Bruise healing.

Remembering,
As life moves through
Time,
May heal because
The vivid present
Can become the
Almost forgotten past.

Age and the Everyday

SOME DAY

Someday I will be old
But not today.

You may look at me
And think I'm there now.
Don't bet on it, Baby,
Still wet behind your ears.

The mind enriched
By years of experience
Explodes with ideas
I could never conjure at
Your tender age.

Gray hair, slack lip,
Halting gait, fading eyes ...
And pulsing imagination,
Rampant with visions!

Just because your skin is firm,
Yours eyes bright,
You think you know the answers.

My dear, it's the questions
That shape your life.
What you find in age
Are the questions.

BEDTIME STORY

With enough wine, I sleep.
But comes two or three o'clock
The urges of age awake me
And then I begin –
A catalogue of day's events,
The guilts of old,
No celebrations.

A circle of thoughts,
The resentment repeats,
And then the lists.

I wrote half a novel
In this late-night hole;
Cried in pain at slights,
Berated someone for
Imagined future hurts.

Prayed a little,
Started over.
Late night circles –
Under my eyes in the morning,
Under my skin forever.

2008

SENIOR MEETING

So many shattered faces,
Age so clearly winning,
as it does.

Old men in wheelchairs,
heads drifting to the chest,
corpulent bodies
overflowing the seat,
no more fancy steps
on the dance floor.
Relaxing into sleep
Or eternal rest.

"Hello. Dinner, sir?"
The eyes open to see
The surrounding world
and let us see
Who is really
Inhabiting this shell.

The wicked blue
Of consciousness,
Ready to engage;
The wit of experience
Ready to be spoken.
Flashes of humor, warmth,

Deep understanding
Until felled
By a stumbling tongue.

The withdrawal of the
Person in front of me,
Clearly accepting the change –
Leaving only the wreckage.

April 2019

SPRING CLEANING

Have you watched 'Hoarders'?
Are you one? Aren't we all?

What else do you call
The pile of cards, papers,
Gifts, single gloves, socks,
Empty boxes in the hall closet?

Shoes are another favorite –
Not shoes but slippers:
Ratty terry, featherless mules,
Clogs with holes in the soles,
Sitting two by one, under the bed,
All the way around.

Here's the glut of
Mandated debris –
Boxes of tax returns,
Check stubs, proofs of
Whatever from wherever.
Better empty boxes.

Cleaning up my life.

2008

AMEN ROSES

I bought a house
with a rose bush.

Not single, prissy buds
but day after day,
bouquets of scent and sight,
blushing richly
over a golden heart.

On the other hand,
in gathering such bounty,
I am scratched,
time and again
by sharp thorns.

But beauty calls for
abandon,
not caution.

So I'll add some red
As I collect my unexpected treasure,
a glory
of sunset roses.

2005

History

JAMESTOWN 2007

Cannon, fife, and drum,
The clop of horses,
Open celebrations at the fort
Against a faint hum
Of our motorized today.

The fort looking new made
Because it is;
In the same old post holes
Dug four hundred years ago.
Tree trunks planted
To enclose the idea of a colony.

Those few men and boys
On sea-battered ships
Brought brave hearts and greed,
White skins and guns,
The idea of laws to live by.

We know a little bit
Of the dark reality
Of sickness, work, famine;
From the dirt-encrusted debris
Dug from graves and dumps.

Squint a little
To glimpse what they saw –
A new world, raw and dangerous,
But theirs by God and the Queen.
And ours too …
Gift of their courage and strength.

Sandy Robinette, "Jamestown 2007", in **Skipping Stones**, *edited by Pete Freas and Anne Meek. (Mindworm Press: Chesapeake, Virginia, 2007), 177. All rights retained by author.*

JAMESTOWN 1607 – 2007

Jamestown celebrated its 400th Anniversary (quadricentennial) in 2007. The first permanent English-speaking settlement on what is now the United States of America began in 1607 on the banks of the James River in Virginia.

Jamestown, the City of Williamsburg, and the State of Virginia planned a month-long schedule of events. The focus was on those early English settlers, the Africans who were a key to prosperity, and the Native Americans who lived in the area.

Queen Elizabeth II and Prince Philip arrived for a Royal Visit in May for the main weekend of ceremonies. (It was the first such State Visit to the U.S. for the Queen since 1991.) Queen Elizabeth II is a direct descendant of James 1, the settlement's namesake.

FOURTH OF JULY
2005

Freedom is a funny thing.
Yours may not be mine
But here we step aside
Enough to let you rant
Or preach or disagree.

Because someone once
Wrote words of power
That were self-evident,
Backed by an army,
Curiously effective,
Despite lack of food, arms, everything.

But with enough
Guts, resolve, eyes to the target;
That dogged determination
Won that war.
We bled again in civil war and
Somehow came back together.
Uneasily but permanently.

We stray, forget, kill,
Wax sentimental, and silly
For something
Called patriotism.

But a core remains.
A rock of gratitude, law,
And common sense.

Our folly bends to judgment
And we keep our freedom.
We give it away.
This legacy freedom
Old as dead heroes.
New each day, each year,
As the world flexes and changes
And always seeks what we offer.

Happy Fourth of July!

Sandy Robinette, "Fourth of July", in **Skipping Stones***, edited by Pete Freas and Anne Meek. (Mindworm Press: Chesapeake, Virginia, 2006), 40. All rights retained by author.*

THE GREAT DISMAL SWAMP FIRE

First the tiny nose tease,
Rich and earthy,
Primitive somehow.

Deep in the earth
The peat rots ...
Old world feel,
Antique smell.

Alive here and now ...
Hot, robust, dense,
Smoke drifts over the edges.

Trees, houses soften
Into dreamscapes,
As the fragrant smoky haze
Slides over fences,

Wraps the porch,
Waits on the doorstep.
Steps softly inside.

Invisible in the corners,
Swamp scent thick as moss,
Layers on today
With long ago mysteries.

2008

Sandy Robinette, "The Great Dismal Swamp Fire," in **The Poet's Domain**, *volume twenty-six, edited by Patricia S. Adler. (Live Wire Press, Charlottesville, Virginia, 2010), 82. All rights returned to the author.*

The Great Dismal Swamp National Wildlife Refuge straddles the Virginia-North Carolina border about thirty miles from my house in Norfolk, Virginia. It is a sprawling 'forested wetland' on the major migratory bird flight paths north and south. This is a recreational gem for those who like to explore black water mystery. Best seen from canoe or kayak, take a guide or compass or you risk being lost once inside among the trees.

This fire started on June 9, 2008 and was thought to be caused by lightning striking the debris from a replanting project of the rare American white cedar, downed during Hurricane Isabel in 2003.

This time 4,884 acres burned in the course of four months. Although a swamp, many areas had deposits of fallen trees and dried out vegetation from a summer drought. Peat deposits which had accumulated over years of natural decay also provided a highly burnable fuel.

Many cultures in similar boggy, swampy areas cut and dry peat for regular use as household fuel. It is considered an early stage of coal. When ignited in the swamp, peat burns deep in the damp soil and is hard to contain. This also contributes to the phenomenon of the water burning.

The smoke produced is dangerous to breathe as it is loaded with particulates.

I did not know any of these facts when I wrote this poem. My personal experience was the daily reminder over those months of a fog of white, the smoke smell, and the feel of something out of the ordinary. Mysteries that remind us that the world has layers we do not notice or understand.

Maybe this poem does too.

FRED HEUTTE, I LOVE YOU

Joy giver,
Planter of trees,
King of the Crape Myrtle.
Fred Heutte,
City Horticulturist
Of Norfolk, Virginia.

By some fortuitous
Luck and certainly
Expertise, he decorated
His city with
Summer glory,
Blossoms everywhere.

Unlike the springtime
Bounty of short-lived
Cherry, pear, and crab apple,
These summertime beauties
Bloomed in the heat
And southern humidity
For months.

Profligate flowers
In the air,
On my car,
Ever before my eyes.
Purple, pink
white, red.
A blessing in
Their everywhere-ness.

Only a bush, you say,
Seeing a newly
planted stem.
Yes,
But turn, turn
And see
The lines of vintage
Trees along most every curb,
in every neighborhood,
Beauty for the entire city.

The trees grow
With dappled bark
That curve and twist
As interesting in
Bare winter as in
The breathtaking
Splendor of summer.

Thank you, Fred Heutte!
Imaginative, wise;
A gift giver of
Holy beauty
For all of us.

FREDERIC HEUTTE
(1899 – 1979)

Frederic Heutte was born in 1899 and, by some serendipity, he became head of Parks for the City of Norfolk from 1937 to 1979.

There is a story before that of course. He was born in Paris to a French father and an American mother. The family returned to the United States and settled on Long Island. He apprenticed in the florist business in New York City and learned even more working on estates in the area. He served in World War I and was stationed in Panama. He added gardening to his duties and was recognized as "the company gardener".

He became a citizen in 1918. Continuing his horticultural career, he worked in a variety of venues. He arrived in Tidewater and, in 1937, became the Superintendent of Parks and Forestry for Norfolk.

In 1938, he and Norfolk City Manager Thomas P. Thompson were granted 74 acres of city owned high, wooded ground plus a 75-acre reservoir adjacent for a city garden. Later that year, under a Works Progress Administration (WPA) grant, 200 African-American women and 20 African-American men were hired to clear the site.

By March of 1939, 4,000 azaleas, 2,000 rhododendrons, 100 bushels of daffodils and several thousand other shrubs and trees had been planted.

This became the Norfolk Botanical Garden, which surrounds the Norfolk International Airport. The Garden has become a national model for reconciling the landscape and commercial aviation.

Fred Heutte leaves a living legacy of thousands of crape myrtle trees along the streets of Norfolk, a renowned Botanical Garden now over 155 acres, and a reputation as a leading advocate for beautification of urban life through landscaping.

Final Thought

WHY WRITE?

When I write a poem,
I don't enclose it
In any form but
My voice.

In my own precise
Mental language,
So you feel
I know you –
Your heart,
Your moment,
As you read.

I don't know you
So how can I do that?
Human, female,
Old, a handful of labels,
Do not give me entrance
At your door.
You do.

Each word should
Mean something,
Naming a reality
Between us.

Or not,
When you slam
Your door.

May 2019

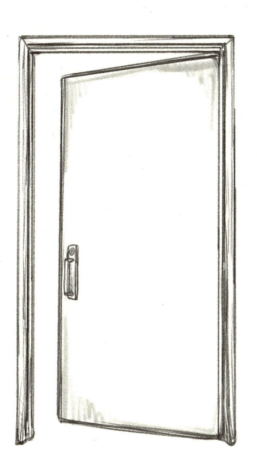

ABOUT THE AUTHOR

Sandy Robinette grew up in suburban Philadelphia as the youngest in a family of seven. Her parents, Angus and Antoinette, located there from New England. Educated through the excellent Philadelphia Diocesan education system, she won a scholarship to Rosemont College (Rosemont, Pennsylvania) and graduated with a B.A. in English Literature.

Sandy married soon after and followed her Naval Officer husband to duty stations on the East, West, and Gulf Coasts. His second career in the federal government took them and their family of eight children to Texas, Ohio, and Northern Virginia.

After his death, Sandy moved to the Tidewater area of Virginia where several of the children and grandchildren lived.

Sandy also discovered a vibrant and welcoming group of authors in the Hampton Roads Writers, Inc. Encouraged by their comments and support, she decided to begin assembling this book of poetry and essays in hope of sharing the comfort and strength she received from Scripture, prayer, and the sacraments in her Church.

Sandy's poetry offers new insights on matters of the heart and the Spirit. She journeys into the layers of life, sometimes hidden in plain sight. She looks at love, joy, weather, sorrow, and the holy places in our hearts.

Sandy has published poetry in several regional anthologies and won a prestigious poetry prize at the recent Hampton Roads Writers Annual Conference competition.

You can contact her at
Sandy.Robinette.poet@gmail.com.
Website: SANDYROBINETTEPOET.WIXSITE.COM/website
Facebook: Sandy Robinette Poet

Photo: ©CRobinette2016. All rights reserved.

*In all circumstances give thanks,
for this is the will of God for you
in Christ Jesus.*
1 Thessalonians 5: 18

©**St. Joseph Edition of
The New American Bible (NAB)**